MIN DEVOTIONAL FOR SPIRITUAL NOURISHMENT

THE WORD TODAY

By Joshua O. Oluwagbemi

THE WORD TODAY VOLUME 02

ISBN-13: 978-978-769-963-8

Publishd by Peace Book Publishing

Printed in the United States of America

Unless otherwise stated all scripture references are taken from the King James Version of the Bible

+234 8034551843 08112949190 08035628305

joshuaolusesanoluwagbemi@gmail.com

gbemijoshua@yahoo.com

DEDICATION

This devotional manual is dedicated to God, the author and giver of inspiration.

ACKNOLEGEMENT

I acknowledge Pastor Mrs Taiwo Oluwagbemi, a dearly beloved wife and a great partner in the kingdom business and all children of God.

TABLE OF CONTENTS

DAY 1

THE PROPHET AND MUSIC MINISTRY

Exodus 15:20-21 "And Miriam the prophetess, the sister of Aaron, took a timbrel in her hand; and all the women went out after her with timbrels and with dances. And Miriam answered them, 'Sing ye to the LORD, for he hath triumphed gloriously; the horse and his rider hath he thrown into the sea."

2 Kings 3:15 "But now bring me a minstrel. And it came to pass, when the minstrel played, that the hand of the LORD came upon him."

Glory be to God in the highest! If you desire growth in your prophetic ministry, cultivating a lifestyle of worship is important.

In our passage today, we see Elisha, the prophet, calling for a minstrel—a singer or musician—to create an atmosphere of worship. As the minstrel played, the hand of the Lord came upon Elisha. Music, especially in the form of poetic praise, has a unique ability to usher in the presence of God and open the door to divine revelation.

The Psalms, written by King David and others, are a testament to this truth. Many are songs of praise, and they carry prophetic declarations. Similarly, Miriam the prophetess understood the power of worship. After God delivered Israel from Pharaoh's army, she took a timbrel, sang, danced, and prophesied.

If you desire to hear from God and operate in the prophetic, cultivate the habit of deep praise and worship, combined with holy living. This combination creates an environment where the Spirit of God can move freely.

We see another example in the early Church in Antioch:

"As they ministered to the Lord, and fasted, the Holy Ghost said, 'Separate me Barnabas and Saul for the work whereunto I have called them." – Acts 13:2

The prophets and teachers at Antioch ministered to the Lord with fasting and worship, and they received clear direction from the Holy Spirit. Worship was central to their relationship with God.

Even Jesus, during His earthly ministry, embraced the power of music and worship. Before His journey to the Mount of Olives, He sang a hymn with His disciples: *"And when they had sung an hymn, they went out into the mount of Olives." – Matthew 26:30*

Music is a powerful bridge between the physical and spiritual realms. The kind of music you engage with influences the inspiration and revelation you receive. Therefore, immerse yourself in worship that glorifies God, and you will experience His divine presence.

Oh Lord, grant us the heart of worship like Miriam, the sons of Asaph, and Elisha. Help us to cultivate a habit of praise that draws us closer to You.

I prophesy restoration and revival over our nation, Nigeria, and the nations of the world. May every dry bone come to life and fulfill Your prophetic mandate. Lord, take over and reign as the Governor among the nations. In Jesus' mighty name, amen.

Spend intentional time in worship today. Choose songs that glorify God and draw you into His presence. Reflect on how music influences your connection with Him and seek His revelation during your time of praise.

God bless you. Amen.

DAY 2

THE ORDEALS OF BEING A PROPHET

Matthew 5:12 *"Rejoice, and be exceeding glad: for great is your reward in heaven: for so persecuted they the prophets which were before you."*

Glory be to God in the highest! As we continue our study on the prophetic ministry, it is important to reflect on the challenges and ordeals faced by those called to be prophets.

Jesus Himself warned that persecution accompanies the prophetic gift. The Greek word *diṓkó* (διώκω) conveys being pursued, harassed, or rejected. The life of a prophet is often marked by trials and tribulations, which refine and test their faith, much like gold in a furnace (the crucible of affliction). One common form of persecution is **rejection**, often starting within one's household or community. Jesus testified, *"A prophet hath no honour in his own country"* (John 4:44). Overfamiliarity breeds contempt. Joseph is a vivid example—his brothers rejected him because of the dreams God gave him.

Another challenge is the perception of **madness**. Jonah's experience illustrates this. When God acts in ways that seem beyond human comprehension, His prophets may appear foolish or even mad to others. The Bible declares: *"That frustrateth the tokens of the liars, and maketh diviners mad; that turneth wise men backward, and maketh their knowledge foolish."* – Isaiah 44:25

Prophets also face the challenge of **speaking truth to power**. Elijah fled from Jezebel's threats, desiring to die in despair (1 Kings 19:4). Jeremiah endured imprisonment and humiliation for proclaiming God's word: *"Then took they Jeremiah, and cast him into the dungeon of Malchiah... and in the dungeon there was no water, but mire: so Jeremiah sank in the mire."* – Jeremiah 38:6

The prophetic ministry often demands acts of obedience that seem **unconventional or uncomfortable** by human standards. For instance:

- Isaiah walked naked and barefoot for three years as a sign to Egypt and Ethiopia (Isaiah 20:3).
- Hosea married an unfaithful wife as a symbolic message to Israel (Hosea 1).
- Agabus bound his hands and feet with Paul's girdle to illustrate Paul's future imprisonment (Acts 21:11).

Another ordeal for prophets is contending with **false or lying spirits**. In *1 Kings 22:22*, the Lord permitted a lying spirit to deceive false prophets, underscoring the need for discernment and faithfulness in delivering God's truth.

Despite these challenges, the reward of obedience far outweighs the suffering. Jesus reminds us: *"Great is your reward in heaven."* Prophets are refined through trials to fulfill God's purpose and glorify His name.

Lord, we thank You for the privilege of serving as vessels for Your word. Grant us the strength to endure trials, the courage to speak truth, and the grace to remain faithful in all circumstances. May we always rejoice, knowing that our reward is eternal.

Bless our nation, Nigeria, and the nations of the world. Let Your truth prevail, and may every prophet You raise walk boldly in their calling. In Jesus' name, amen.

Reflect on how you handle rejection or trials in your own life. Ask God for the strength to stand firm, even when misunderstood or persecuted. Seek His wisdom in all that you do, trusting His purpose in your journey.

God bless you. Amen.

DAY 3

THE PROPHET AND THE WORD OF GOD

1 Samuel 3:10 *"And the LORD came, and stood, and called as at other times, Samuel, Samuel. Then Samuel answered, 'Speak; for thy servant heareth."*

Glory be to God in the highest! As we continue our study on the ministries of the prophet, it is vital to understand the deep connection between the prophet and the Word of God. The Church itself is built on the foundation of the apostles and prophets, with Jesus Christ as the cornerstone: *"And are built upon the foundation of the apostles and prophets, Jesus Christ himself being the chief cornerstone." – Ephesians 2:20*

This prophetic foundation reminds us that everyone born of water and the Spirit carries a prophetic anointing to some degree. However, the depth of this anointing depends on how closely one walks with God.

Our text today offers one of the most profound and humbling scenes in Scripture. God, who shows no favoritism, bypassed Eli—the high priest—and his corrupt sons, Hophni and Phinehas. Instead, He called Samuel, a young and inexperienced boy, to carry His Word. Why? Because

Samuel valued God's commandments, unlike Eli, who had forsaken them.

Before this pivotal moment, Scripture paints a troubling picture of the state of Israel's spiritual leadership: *"And the child Samuel ministered unto the LORD before Eli. And the word of the LORD was precious in those days; there was no open vision."* – *1 Samuel 3:1*

What a sobering reality! The Word of God was rare, and there was no open vision. Yet people continued to come to Shiloh, the seat of the Ark of the Covenant, seeking spiritual guidance from Eli and his sons. One can only imagine the kind of empty words or misguided counsel they received.

A true prophet is a person of the Word. They live, abide in, and love the Word of God. Just as Mary chose to sit at Jesus' feet and listen to His teaching, prophets prioritize the Word over distractions, unlike Martha, who was cumbered with much serving (Luke 10:38-42).

When Eli failed to obey God's Word, God turned to Samuel. Eli, to his credit, taught Samuel how to respond when God called: *"Speak, for thy servant heareth."*

This is a lesson for all of us. Cherish the Word, and He will speak to you. Obey the Word, and your strength will increase. Love the Word, and God will reveal His secrets to you, just as He did with Abraham.

In the Old Testament, the Word of the Lord would come to prophets like Jeremiah: *"The word of the LORD came also unto me, saying…" – Jeremiah 16:1*

But today, the Word has become flesh and now dwells within us (John 1:14). As believers, we have the Word living inside us through the Spirit. This truth confirms that you, too, are a prophet in one way or another.

Oh God, the Spirit of the prophets, breathe upon us through Your Word. Like Samuel, may we hear and respond to Your voice. Pour out Your Spirit upon all flesh as You promised in *Joel 2:28*. Reveal Your Word to us, and help us to walk in obedience and faithfulness. In Jesus Christ's mighty name, amen.

Spend time meditating on a specific Scripture today. Ask God to reveal Himself to you through His Word and to strengthen your prophetic calling. Listen for His voice and be ready to respond, saying, *"Speak, Lord, for Your servant hears."* God bless you. Amen.

DAY 4

THE OLD AND THE YOUNG PROPHETS

1 Kings 13:26, 30 "And when the prophet that brought him back from the way heard thereof, he said, 'It is the man of God, who was disobedient unto the word of the LORD: therefore the LORD hath delivered him unto the lion, which hath torn him, and slain him, according to the word of the LORD, which he spake unto him.' ... And he laid his carcase in his own grave; and they mourned over him, saying, 'Alas, my brother!'"

Glory be to God in the highest for the beloved brothers and sisters in our lives who wish us well and desire to see us prosper spiritually and in all areas of life. May their labor of love be richly rewarded, in Jesus' mighty name.

Today's text recounts one of the most heart-wrenching stories in Scripture: the tragic tale of the young prophet from Judah and his encounter with the old prophet. The young prophet, obediently following God's word, was deceived and ultimately met his untimely death.

What caused such a tragic event? **Envy**.

The old prophet, instead of encouraging his younger colleague, became an agent of destruction. His envy led him to lie, manipulate, and ultimately cause the young prophet's downfall. It's sobering to consider that someone from the same prophetic league—a fellow servant of God—could act in such a way.

Envy, as Scripture warns, is a dangerous and destructive force. The Apostle James cautions: "*But if ye have bitter envying and strife in your hearts, glory not, and lie not against the truth. For where envying and strife is, there is confusion and every evil work.*" – James 3:14, 16

Solomon echoes this warning: "*Wrath is cruel, and anger is outrageous; but who is able to stand before envy?*" – Proverbs 27:4

Envy blinds us to the good in others and turns potential allies into rivals. It poisons relationships and leads to actions that grieve God's heart. The old prophet, instead of mentoring the young man of God or celebrating his obedience, allowed bitterness to turn him into a stumbling block.

We are called to be like Moses, who rejoiced in others' spiritual growth and supported God's work in the lives of his brethren. Instead of tearing others down, we should lift them up, nurturing their God-given potential and celebrating their successes.

Heavenly Father, we ask for Your grace to guard our hearts

against envy and strife. Help us to celebrate the gifts and successes of others, rejoicing in the good You are doing through them.

For those who are victims of envious acts, Lord, deliver them from every satanic plot meant to destroy their purpose. May the works of their hands and the glory of their labor be preserved, in Jesus Christ's mighty name. Amen.

Reflect on your relationships today. Are you harboring envy or bitterness toward someone's success? Surrender it to God and ask Him to fill your heart with love, encouragement, and a spirit of unity. Take a step to support or encourage someone you admire, celebrating their progress in the Lord.

God bless you. Amen

DAY 5

PROPHET'S REWARD

Matthew 10:41 "He that receiveth a prophet in the name of a prophet shall receive a prophet's reward; and he that receiveth a righteous man in the name of a righteous man shall receive a righteous man's reward."

Proverbs 18:16 "A man's gift maketh room for him, and bringeth him before great men."

Glory be to God in the Highest! Scripture reminds us that the gift of a man makes room for him, granting him access to influential circles. Every true prophet carries influence—spiritual and, often, societal. A prophet's anointing opens doors not only for divine revelations but also for tangible transformations in their lives and the lives of others.

Let's take a closer look at the prophet's reward through the lives of biblical examples:

Joseph's gift of interpreting dreams elevated him to prominence. In Genesis 41, his ability to discern and articulate Pharaoh's dreams resulted in ten major life changes in a single day:

He was released unconditionally from imprisonment, clearing him of false accusations, He was clothed with garments signifying restoration and honor, Pharaoh gave him a royal signet ring as a mark of authority, A golden necklace was placed on him, symbolizing wealth and prestige, Joseph was appointed Prime Minister of Egypt, second only to Pharaoh, He was granted royal accommodations and privileges, including an official chariot, He was given a new name, **Zaphnathpaaneah**, signifying his new identity and purpose, Pharaoh arranged his marriage to Asenath, a woman of beauty and stature, He rode in Pharaoh's second chariot as a sign of his elevated position, His words carried the weight of law and authority across Egypt.

What an extraordinary testimony of how a prophetic gift can transform one's destiny!

Elisha's prophetic ministry brought him into contact with kings, military leaders, and influential figures. In 2 Kings 4:13, Elisha offers to advocate for the Shunammite woman before the king and the army commander, demonstrating his widespread connections. His influence extended to political, military, and economic spheres, proving that a prophet's reward often includes access and opportunities to effect change.

Daniel's prophetic gift made him a leader across multiple empires, including Babylon, Persia, and Media. His God-given wisdom and ability to interpret dreams ensured his relevance in every kingdom he served. Furthermore, his prophetic anointing elevated his friends—Hananiah, Mishael, and Azariah (Shadrach, Meshach, and Abednego)—to positions of prominence.

Jesus, the ultimate prophet, embodied the Spirit of Prophecy. Through Him, we are instructed to desire prophetic gifts: "Wherefore, brethren, covet to prophesy, and forbid not to speak with tongues."1 Corinthians 14:39

As believers, we are called to embrace this anointing, allowing God to work through us to impact our generation.

Lord Jesus Christ, Spirit of the Prophets, we ask You to stir up the prophetic anointing in us today. Let our gifts make room for us and grant us relevance in our generation. May we walk in obedience, humility, and boldness, knowing that You reward those who remain faithful. We thank You for the lessons in this series, Lord. To You be all the glory!

Take time today to reflect on the gifts God has placed in your life. Are you using them for His glory? Pray for God to open doors of influence and opportunity, and be ready to walk boldly into them when they come.

God bless you. Amen.

DAY 6

DISOBEDIENCE – THE PITFALL OF THE PROPHETS

1 Kings 13:21-22 "And he cried unto the man of God that came from Judah, saying, Thus saith the LORD, Forasmuch as thou hast disobeyed the mouth of the LORD, and hast not kept the commandment which the LORD thy God commanded thee... thy carcase shall not come unto the sepulchre of thy fathers."

Glory be to God in the Highest! The story of the young prophet from Judah is a sobering lesson for every believer. This was a man chosen by God, carrying divine instruction to prophesy against King Jeroboam's idolatry. However, his downfall came through disobedience—not because of external persecution, but due to deception from an "old prophet."

Let's examine the key points of this account:

Divine Instructions The young prophet was given clear directives from God: He was not to eat or drink while in Bethel.He was to return by a different route than the one he took to arrive. (1 Kings 13:17). His obedience to these instructions was essential, as they were directly tied to his prophetic mission.

The Trap of the Old Prophet An old prophet, living in Bethel, deceived the young man with a fabricated message, claiming, *"I am a prophet also as thou art; and an angel spake unto me by the word of the LORD." (1 Kings 13:18*). Tragically, the young prophet believed the lie and disobeyed God's command.

This incident highlights a critical danger: **not every "prophet" carries the truth of God.** The old prophet, driven by envy or curiosity, became a stumbling block to the young prophet's mission.

The Consequences of Disobedience Despite his initial great exploit in delivering God's message to Jeroboam, the young prophet's failure to obey God's word led to his death. A lion killed him on the way home, marking the tragic end of his ministry. (*1 Kings 13:24*)

The story reminds us of the presence of "old prophets" in every generation—individuals who may mislead, whether out of envy, ignorance, or malice. As *1 John 4:1* warns: *"Beloved, believe not every spirit, but try the spirits whether they are of God: because many false prophets are gone out into the world."*

We are called to test every spirit using the Word of God as our standard. Anything that contradicts His Word is not from Him.

False prophets can wreak havoc in families, marriages, and personal lives, as seen in many modern-day examples. One such story involved a "prophet" prescribing inappropriate and harmful actions to a woman seeking the fruit of the womb. Such acts are not from God but are works of deception designed to derail faith.

Partial obedience is disobedience. The young prophet succeeded in delivering his message but failed in adhering to the full instructions of God. We must remember that our faithfulness to God is measured by our adherence to His commands, not just our accomplishments.

Oh Lion of the Tribe of Judah, help us to remain steadfast in Your Word, no matter the challenges or distractions around us. Preserve us from the deception of false prophets and their schemes. Grant us discernment to test every spirit and the courage to obey Your commands completely. Strengthen us, Lord, to remain faithful on our journey, so that we may fulfill Your purpose for our lives. In Jesus Christ's mighty name, we pray. Amen.

Take time to reflect on your spiritual influences. Are you discerning the voices you listen to? Spend time in God's Word and ask the Holy Spirit to guide you in distinguishing truth from deception.

God bless you. Amen.

DAY 7

GOOD HUMAN RELATIONS IS A MUST IN THE JOURNEY OF DESTINY

Acts 10:38 *"How God anointed Jesus of Nazareth with the Holy Ghost and with power: who went about doing good, and healing all that were oppressed of the devil; for God was with him."*

2 Peter 1:5–9 *"And beside this, giving all diligence, add to your faith virtue; and to virtue knowledge; and to knowledge temperance; and to temperance patience; and to patience godliness; and to godliness brotherly kindness; and to brotherly kindness charity. For if these things be in you, and abound, they make you that ye shall neither be barren nor unfruitful in the knowledge of our Lord Jesus Christ. But he that lacketh these things is blind, and cannot see afar off, and hath forgotten that he was purged from his old sins."*

Glory be to God in the Highest! In the journey of destiny, it is imperative to imbibe and maintain the culture of good human relations with as many people as we come across daily. This was one of the outstanding attributes of Jesus Christ Himself during His earthly ministry. He went about doing good, not to please men, but as an expression of His divine nature as the good God.

Those who fulfill destiny are individuals who practice good human relations. Throughout history, every individual who achieved great things was helped by God through the people around them. Joseph exemplifies this truth. Despite finding himself in the challenging environment of a dungeon, he maintained excellent relationships with prison officials and fellow inmates. His good character earned him the position of overseer in the prison, putting him in charge of everything. There is no record of Joseph creating enemies for himself, even in adversity. Today, many forget the importance of treating others well, especially when they are in positions of privilege or power. Such individuals act as if there is no tomorrow, forgetting the lessons of humility.

The story of General Naaman also illustrates the importance of good human relations. His healing from leprosy became possible because of the love and respect he showed to a young slave girl. She was so moved by his kindness that she recommended the prophet Elisha as the solution to his health challenges. Naaman's humility in listening to her advice and that of his other servants led him to obey Elisha's instructions and receive his miracle. This story highlights how compassion and respect for others can open doors to divine blessings.

In human relationships lies the goodness of God. No matter

our circumstances, we are called to do good to everyone we encounter, especially the less privileged. Dorcas, also known as Tabitha, is another powerful example of someone who lived a life of kindness and compassion. Her good deeds, particularly to widows, were so impactful that God restored her to life when she died. This was a testament to the power of good human relations and the divine rewards that come with them.

However, it is heartbreaking that oppression has become rampant in many communities, including within the Church. It is contrary to Christ's teachings to live a life that oppresses or mistreats others. Instead, believers are called to uplift and support one another, ensuring that their actions reflect the love of Christ.

If you truly desire to walk in the light of Christ, you must ask yourself whether heaven can testify that you go about doing good as Jesus did. Are you known for your kindness and compassion toward others?

In our journey through life, help us, Lord, to always value the people around us, especially the vulnerable and less privileged. Grant us the grace to maintain good human relations and reflect Your goodness in all our dealings. May our actions honor You, in Jesus' name. Amen.

Let your life be a light, shining kindness into the world.

God bless you. Amen.

32

DAY 8

UNDER THE JUNIPER TREE

1 Kings 19:4 *"But he himself went a day's journey into the wilderness, and came and sat down under a juniper tree: and he requested for himself that he might die; and said, It is enough; now, O LORD, take away my life; for I am not better than my fathers."*

Glory be to God in the Highest, for He is our hiding place and shelter in times of storm!

After Elijah's extraordinary victory on Mount Carmel, where he called down fire from heaven and exposed the false prophets of Baal, one would not expect the mighty prophet to fall into fear and despair. Yet, when Jezebel, the wicked queen, threatened his life, Elijah fled. This prophet, endowed with immense power, capable of commanding the elements, suddenly found himself running into the wilderness, sitting under a juniper tree, despondent and wishing for death.

Elijah's fear and discouragement seemed illogical given his recent triumph, but it reflects a common experience. Despite witnessing God's power in the past, we often falter in the face of fresh challenges. Elijah believed his efforts had been futile, thinking he was the only faithful servant of God left, and his miraculous works had made no impact on Israel's spiritual condition.

Jezebel's terror was a testament to her reputation as a ruthless, unyielding adversary of God's people. Her threats magnified Elijah's despair, convincing him that death was imminent. In his disheartened state, Elijah forgot that the same God who brought fire down from heaven could protect him from Jezebel.

Many believers today find themselves under their own "juniper tree," overwhelmed by fear, discouragement, and the weight of unmet expectations. Like Elijah, they flee to the wilderness of depression and hopelessness, convinced that their situations are beyond redemption. Yet, God remains constant. The power that sustained you in past victories is still available today. *"Jesus Christ the same yesterday, and today, and forever." – Hebrews 13:8.*

The psalmist provides a remedy for moments like these: *"Why art thou cast down, O my soul? and why art thou disquieted in me? hope thou in God: for I shall yet praise him for the help of his countenance." – Psalm 42:5-6.* King David, too, experienced moments of despair. When Ziklag was attacked, and his family and possessions were taken, he wept until he had no strength left. Yet, he found encouragement by turning to God.

When life feels overwhelming, remember to tell your soul

to hope in God. Recall His faithfulness in past trials and praise Him for the deliverance He will bring.

Lord, help us to trust in You even when fear and despair threaten to consume us. Strengthen our faith and remind us of Your constant presence and power. We choose to hope in You and praise You for Your help and guidance. In Jesus' name, Amen.

Identify an area in your life where fear or discouragement has taken root. Speak to your soul today, just as the psalmist did, and declare, "Hope in God!" Write down three ways God has been faithful to you in the past, and meditate on them throughout the day. Share your testimony with someone who may also need encouragement.

Hold on, beloved. The God of wonders remains with you, and He will see you through.

God bless you. Amen.

DAY 9

ACCUSATION OVERULES

1 Kings 19:14-15, 18 "And he said, I have been very jealous for the LORD God of hosts: because the children of Israel have forsaken thy covenant, thrown down thine altars, and slain thy prophets with the sword; and I, even I only, am left; and they seek my life, to take it away. And the LORD said unto him, Go, return on thy way to the wilderness of Damascus: and when thou comest, anoint Hazael to be king over Syria. Yet I have left me seven thousand in Israel, all the knees which have not bowed unto Baal, and every mouth which hath not kissed him."

Glory be to God in the Highest!

Accusation is a powerful weapon that can skew perspectives and derail purpose. In today's reading, Elijah, though a mighty prophet, succumbs to despair and frustration. He levels a charge against Israel, claiming that they have forsaken God and that he alone remains faithful. However, God, in His omniscience, corrects Elijah's narrow perspective by revealing the existence of 7,000 faithful servants who have neither bowed to Baal nor kissed him.

Unlike Moses, who interceded for Israel despite their rebellion, Elijah's despair led him to accuse rather than advocate.

As a result, God directs him to anoint others to carry out tasks he was unwilling or unable to complete.

This moment serves as a reminder that human perceptions are often limited. In times of frustration, we may fail to see the bigger picture or the hidden workings of God. It also warns us of the danger of self-righteousness—thinking we alone are doing God's will while others are failing.

Lord, forgive us for the times We have accused or judged others unfairly. Help is to see as You see and to trust in Your plans, even when circumstances seem bleak. Use me as an instrument of Your mercy and restoration in my generation. May my words and actions bring healing, encouragement, and hope to those around me. In Jesus' name, Amen.

Examine your role in your community or ministry today. Are you a builder who intercedes on behalf of others, or have you fallen into the trap of being an accuser of the brethren? Ask God to open your eyes to the hidden faithful around you and to grant you the humility to serve with a spirit of grace and compassion.

God bless you. Amen.

DAY 10

PROPHECY: A PROMISE OF THE FATHER

Joel 2:28 *"And it shall come to pass afterward, that I will pour out my spirit upon all flesh; and your sons and your daughters shall prophesy, your old men shall dream dreams, your young men shall see visions."*

Glory be to God in the Highest for His unfailing promises! The prophecy of Joel stands as a beacon of hope and empowerment for the Church, spanning from the day of Pentecost to the present age. Joel envisioned a time when the Holy Spirit would not be limited to prophets, priests, or kings but would be poured out upon all flesh—young and old, male and female, rich and poor.

The word "pour out" in the original Hebrew is שָׁפַךְ (shafakh), meaning to spill or gush forth abundantly. God promised to pour out His רוּחַ (ruach), meaning Spirit or breath, on כָּל־בָּשָׂר (kol basar), meaning "all flesh," indicating that this gift is for everyone, without exceptions.

This prophecy was fulfilled in Acts 2 when the Holy Spirit descended upon the early believers, marking the birth of the Church.

This divine outpouring is not a one-time event but a continuous promise for every believer across generations. However, in today's world, many have neglected this promise. Youths chase fleeting pleasures, while older generations struggle to tap into the fullness of God's Spirit. The result is a spiritual barrenness that stifles visions, dreams, and the gift of prophecy.

Now more than ever, the Church must cry out for a fresh outpouring of the Holy Spirit. It is through the Spirit that we gain insight, direction, and power to fulfill our divine mandate.

Come, Holy Spirit! Pour out Your presence upon us anew. Ignite the hearts of our youths to seek Your face and embrace Your gifts. Restore the dreams and visions of the aged. Lord, let there be a fresh Pentecost in our lives, churches, and nations. We long for Your power and guidance to navigate these dark times. In Jesus' name, Amen.

Take time today to seek a personal encounter with the Holy Spirit. Let your heart be open to receive His outpouring afresh.

God bless you. Amen.

DAY 11

THE SOUL TRADERS

Acts 16:16-17, 19 "*And it came to pass, as we went to prayer, a certain damsel possessed with a spirit of divination met us, which brought her masters much gain by soothsaying: The same followed Paul and us, and cried, saying, These men are the servants of the most high God, which shew unto us the way of salvation. And when her masters saw that the hope of their gains was gone, they caught Paul and Silas, and drew them into the marketplace unto the rulers.*"

Glory be to God in the Highest! Today, we confront a stark reality: modern-day slavery of the soul. Satan, the master deceiver, is deeply invested in trading souls. From the beginning, the soul of man has been a prized possession. Genesis 2:7 reveals that man became a living soul through the breath of God, and since then, the soul has remained the core of human existence.

The devil's strategy is clear: to enslave and exchange souls under the guise of wealth, fame, and power. Jesus Himself warned in *Matthew 16:26* of the futility of gaining the world at the cost of one's soul. Satan's business thrives in this era, where people sacrifice their eternal destiny for temporal pleasures. The text in *Revelation 18:12-13* lists "souls of men" as merchandise, highlighting the devil's cruel trade.

In Acts 16, we see a young girl enslaved by a spirit of divination. She was exploited by her masters for financial gain, much like how false prophets, money ritualists, and occultic societies exploit people today. Their ultimate goal aligns with Satan's agenda—to drag as many souls to hell as possible.

Yet, God's desire is to save and secure every soul for eternity. Through Christ, the price for our redemption has been fully paid.

Heavenly Father, we thank You for the priceless gift of our souls. Help us to guard them diligently and resist the traps of the enemy. We declare liberty over every soul in captivity, breaking the chains of pseudo-Christianity, false doctrines, and deceitful practices. Keep us steadfast in You, and may we never lose sight of our eternal inheritance. In Jesus' name, Amen.

Examine your life. Are you trading your soul for the fleeting pleasures of this world? Have you been lured into spiritual captivity under the guise of false promises? Today, take a stand. Break free from every form of soul enslavement and refuse to compromise your eternal destiny for temporary gain.

God bless you. Amen.

DAY 12

SOUL WINNING

Acts 1:8-9 *"But ye shall receive power, after that the Holy Ghost is come upon you: and ye shall be witnesses unto me both in Jerusalem, and in all Judaea, and in Samaria, and unto the uttermost part of the earth. And when he had spoken these things, while they beheld, he was taken up; and a cloud received him out of their sight."*

2 Timothy 4:5 *"But watch thou in all things, endure afflictions, do the work of an evangelist, make full proof of thy ministry."*

Glory be to God in the Highest for the call to the ministry of soul winning! Since the fall of man in the Garden of Eden, God's heart has longed for the reconciliation of humanity. He has entrusted us with the ministry of reconciliation through Christ. As stated in 2 Corinthians 5:18-19, God works through us to bring the lost back to Him, reconciling the world through the message of salvation.

Soul winning, therefore, is not just a church activity but the heartbeat of God. It is the essence of the Great Commission given by Christ to His disciples and by extension to us. We are **saved to save others.**

Unfortunately, many believers have misplaced priorities. Resources are poured into building beautiful church edifices, purchasing mission buses, and organizing elaborate programs, yet the core mandate of evangelism is often neglected. Souls perish daily, and few are concerned about their eternal fate. The charge given to Timothy by Paul is one we must take seriously: *"Do the work of an evangelist."*

The harvest is indeed plentiful, but the laborers are few. The blood of unsaved souls will be required of us if we fail to share the gospel.

Lord, help us to set our priorities right. Stir in our hearts a passion for soul winning. Let the burden of the Great Commission consume us. Grant us the boldness and wisdom to reach out to the lost, that we may reconcile them to You through Christ. In Jesus' mighty name, Amen.

Reach out to one soul today. Make soul-winning a priority in your life. Whether through personal evangelism, supporting mission work, or interceding for the lost, commit yourself to the ministry of reconciliation.

God bless you. Amen.

DAY 13

RESCUE THE PERISHING: A COMMAND TO US ALL FOR DUTY DEMANDS IT

Proverbs 11:30 *"The fruit of the righteous is a tree of life; and he that winneth souls is wise."*

Glory be to God! Today, we meditate on the powerful call to **rescue the perishing**, inspired by the timeless hymn penned by **Fanny J. Crosby**. This hymn encapsulates the heart of soul-winning: reaching out in love and compassion to those lost in sin, sharing with them the message of Jesus Christ, the mighty Savior.

1. Rescue the perishing,
Care for the dying,
Snatch them in pity from sin and the grave;
Weep o'er the erring one,
Lift up the fallen,
Tell them of Jesus the mighty to save. Rescue the perishing,
Care for the dying;
Jesus is merciful,
 Jesus will save.

2. Though they are slighting Him,
Still He is waiting,
Waiting the penitent child to receive;
Plead with them earnestly,
Plead with them gently;
He will forgive if they only believe.

3. Down in the human heart,
Crushed by the tempter,

Feelings lie buried that grace can restore;
Touched by a loving heart,
Wakened by kindness,
Chords that are broken will vibrate once more.
4. Rescue the perishing,

Duty demands it;
Strength for thy labor the Lord will provide;
Back to the narrow way,
Patiently win them;
Tell the poor wand'rer a Savior has died.

As I listened to this heartfelt hymn, led by the prompting of the Holy Spirit, I was deeply moved to tears. It wasn't the melody or harmony that touched me, but the powerful words and message that resonated deeply with our church community at this time.

Crosby's words remind us that the lost are not only within our reach but also beyond the church walls. They are in places of brokenness, burdened by sin, and yearning for hope. Many are crushed by the weight of life's temptations and trials, their hearts buried under layers of despair. Yet, a touch of grace and kindness can revive their spirits and lead them back to life in Christ.

The hymn's final stanza highlights the urgency of this mission: *"Rescue the perishing, duty demands it."* Soul-winning is not an optional activity; it is a **command** given to all believers. As soldiers in the Lord's army, we are called to leave our comfort zones and reach out to the lost, just as Peter did when he obeyed the Spirit's call to go to Cornelius' household in Acts 10.

The fields are indeed ripe for harvest. Souls are waiting to hear the good news, and the Lord is counting on us to be His hands and feet.

Today, let the words of this hymn inspire you to action. Seek out those who are perishing—whether it be a neighbor, a colleague, or even a stranger—and share with them the life-saving message of Jesus.

Lord, we thank You for the privilege of partnering with You in the ministry of soul-winning. Stir in our hearts a deep compassion for the lost. Strengthen us for the task, and make us faithful ambassadors of Your love. Use us to bring light to those in darkness and to rescue the perishing. In Jesus' mighty name, Amen.

Reach out to a soul today. God bless you richly.

DAY 14

MUST I GO EMPTY-HANDED? JUST A SOUL TO GREET HIM

Daniel 12:3 "And they that be wise shall shine as the brightness of the firmament; and they that turn many to righteousness as the stars for ever and ever."

1 Thessalonians 2:19 "For what is our hope, or joy, or crown of rejoicing? Are not even ye in the presence of our Lord Jesus Chrisqt at his coming?

Glory be to God in the Highest! Today's reflection calls us to examine the purpose of our lives and our readiness to meet Jesus. The hymn *"Must I Go, and Empty-Handed"* by Charles C. Luther was born from the heartbreaking story of a young woman on her deathbed. Though she had recently received salvation, her sorrow came from realizing she had no time left to win souls for Christ. Her question, "Must I go and empty-handed?" inspired this powerful hymn, reminding us of the eternal importance of soul-winning.

The words of the hymn resonate deeply:

Must I go, and empty-handed,
Thus my dear Redeemer meet?
Not one day of service give Him,
Lay no trophy at His feet?

This is a challenge to every believer. Daniel 12:3 promises that those who lead others to righteousness will shine like stars forever. In 1 Thessalonians 2:19, Paul refers to the people he has won to Christ as his crown of rejoicing. These scriptures emphasize that the greatest reward in heaven will not be material wealth but the souls we bring to Christ.

The thought of standing before Jesus without having led anyone to Him is a sobering one. Time is short, and the opportunity to reach others with the gospel is now. The young woman's regret should stir us to action. She wished for just one more chance to share her faith, but for us, that chance is still available. Jesus Himself said, *"The night cometh, when no man can work" —John 9:4.*

As we reflect on this hymn and the story behind it, it is clear that our lives should be focused on fulfilling the Great Commission. The call to rescue souls is not just for pastors or missionaries but for every believer. Each of us has a role in sharing the good news, whether through words, actions, or simply living a life that reflects Christ's love.

Let us consider the urgency of this task. The fields are ripe for harvest, but laborers are few. Today is the day to reach out to someone, to share the message of salvation, and to plant seeds of hope. Every soul matters to God, and every effort to lead someone to Christ is a victory in heaven.

Lord Jesus, we pray for the grace to be faithful ambassadors of Your gospel. May we never stand before You empty-handed. Open our eyes to the opportunities around us and give us the boldness to speak Your truth. Help us to invest our time, resources, and energy in what truly matters—bringing souls into Your kingdom. Strengthen us for this task, and may we shine as lights in a dark world. In Your mighty name, we pray. Amen.

Today, take a step of faith. Reach out to someone with the message of salvation. Let no opportunity pass without sharing the love of Christ. A crown of rejoicing awaits those who turn many to righteousness. God bless you as you labor for His glory.

God bless you. Amen.

DAY 15

YOU ARE A WATCHMAN

Ezekiel 3:16-19 *"Son of man, I have made thee a watchman unto the house of Israel: therefore hear the word at my mouth, and give them warning from me... When I say unto the wicked, Thou shalt surely die; and thou givest him not warning... his blood will I require at thine hand."*

Glory be to God in the Highest! Today's reflection is a solemn reminder of our divine assignment as watchmen. God's word to Ezekiel highlights the weight of responsibility entrusted to us: to warn, guide, and point others to salvation. The role of a watchman is not optional—it is a charge given to every believer.

Being a watchman means standing guard over souls, keeping them from the dangers of eternal separation from God. The consequences of neglecting this duty are severe. Just as Ezekiel was held accountable for failing to warn the wicked, we too will be accountable for those we could have reached but didn't.

2 Corinthians 5:11 reminds us of the seriousness of our mission: *"Knowing therefore the terror of the Lord, we persuade men."* The reality of hell is not a myth—it is as real as the molten lava beneath the earth. Ignorance of this truth will not excuse us on the day of judgment.

Consider the tragic example of Eli, the high priest. He did not personally commit grievous sins but failed in his duty to correct and warn his sons. His negligence led to their downfall and his own demise. *1 Samuel 3:13* declares, *"Because his sons made themselves vile, and he restrained them not."* Eli's passive attitude—his failure to act as a watchman—brought about judgment on his household.

We must not adopt the spirit of Eli, the "I-don't-care" attitude. Instead, we must take up the mantle of responsibility, starting with those closest to us. Our mission begins in our personal "Jerusalem"—our families, friends, and communities—and extends to the ends of the earth.

Matthew 10:7-8 gives clear instructions: *"As ye go, preach, saying, The kingdom of heaven is at hand. Heal the sick, cleanse the lepers, raise the dead, cast out devils: freely ye have received, freely give."* The gospel is not to be commercialized but freely shared, for it is a message of life and hope.

There are no barriers to being a watchman—no age, title, race, or gender restrictions. It is a call for all who have received salvation. Our duty is to proclaim the good news, warn of the dangers of sin, and bring as many as possible into the fold of Christ.

May we not be found guilty of the blood of others due to negligence. Instead, let us take up the charge with urgency and passion. The words of Charles Wesley resonate here: *"Our gracious Master and my King, assist us to proclaim, to spread through all the earth abroad, the honors of Thy name."*

Lord Jesus, help us to be faithful watchmen, diligent in our calling to warn and save souls. Remove every spirit of complacency and grant us boldness to proclaim Your truth. Strengthen us to fulfill this divine duty with love and urgency. In Your mighty name, we pray. Amen.

Today, let us reflect on the lives within our reach and commit to sharing the gospel with at least one person. A soul is waiting for your voice—be the watchman they need.

God bless you. Amen.

DAY 16

A MOBILE PULPIT

Matthew 4:19 *"Follow me, and I will make you fishers of men."*

Mark 1:17 *"Come ye after me, and I will make you to become fishers of men."*

Acts 5:42 *"And daily in the temple, and in every house, they ceased not to teach and preach Jesus Christ."*

Glory be to God in the Highest, amen and amen!

Today's reflection is centered on the concept of a **mobile pulpit**—a flexible and dynamic platform for spreading the gospel. Fishing, as Jesus metaphorically used, is not a passive endeavor. A fisherman moves from place to place, employing different tools and strategies to catch fish. Similarly, we are called to be *"fishers of men,"* ready to go wherever souls are in need of salvation.

A pulpit is traditionally seen as a fixed platform where sermons are delivered, but in the context of soul-winning, it must be mobile and adaptable. It represents any place from which we can proclaim the Word of God—whether it be a church altar, a street corner, a market, a correctional facility, or a media platform. The early apostles understood this well, as *Acts 5:42* reveals that they preached daily, not just in temples but also from house to house.

Beloved, the call to evangelism demands flexibility. We cannot be confined to physical structures. Jesus' instruction to His disciples was clear: *"Go ye into all the world"* (Mark 16:15). The pulpit, therefore, extends to every place where souls can be reached.

Consider the example of the late Archbishop Olumakaiye, who took the gospel to parks, joints, and public spaces across Lagos Island. His commitment to a mobile pulpit was a testament to his understanding that evangelism is not limited to church walls.

In today's world, our pulpit can be digital—through radio, television, social media, and online platforms. Every believer is a carrier of God's message, and our jurisdiction is global. We are called to use every available means to spread the gospel, just as fishermen use nets, hooks, and trawlers to catch fish.

Father, in the name of Jesus Christ, grant us the grace to carry Your Word beyond the confines of our comfort zones. Help us to be flexible and bold in proclaiming the gospel wherever souls need salvation. Empower us to be effective fishers of men, using every platform available to reach the lost. Amen.

Let us embrace the mindset of a mobile pulpit. Whether in our workplaces, communities, or digital spaces, we are ambassadors of Christ. The task may seem daunting, but Jesus assures us that He will make us "fishers of men." He equips those He calls.

God bless you richly as you take the gospel to new places today. Remember, the whole world is your mission field.

DAY 17

SPEND AND BE SPENT — BARNABAS: A CASE STUDY

Acts 4:36-37 *"And Joses, who by the apostles was sur-named Barnabas, (which is, being interpreted, The son of consolation,) a Levite, and of the country of Cyprus, having land, sold it, and brought the money, and laid it at the apostles' feet."*

Acts 12:24-25 *"But the word of God grew and multiplied. And Barnabas and Saul returned from Jerusalem, when they had fulfilled their ministry, and took with them John, whose surname was Mark."*

"My gracious Master and my God,
Assist me to proclaim,
To spread through all the earth abroad,
The honors of Thy name." — C. Wesley

Glory be to God in the Highest, from whom all blessings flow! Amen and amen.

Today, we reflect on the life of a remarkable man of faith: Joses, later known as Barnabas, meaning "Son of Consolation." A Levite from Cyprus, Barnabas stands out in the early Church not just for his faith but for his sacrificial giving and active participation in God's mission.

Barnabas saw a need in the young Church and responded by selling his land, bringing the proceeds to the apostles' feet. This act of selflessness was not about seeking recognition but about advancing the gospel. His generosity earned him the title "Son of Consolation," as his giving brought comfort and support to the growing Christian community. Barnabas could have used his wealth for personal gain or pleasure, but he chose to **spend and be spent** for the sake of Christ. His actions remind us that financial resources play a crucial role in spreading the gospel, yet it is not only about money. Barnabas also gave his time, energy, and life to the mission, becoming a teacher, preacher, and encourager. He introduced Paul to the apostles, mentored young believers, and partnered in missionary journeys, as seen in Acts 11:22-26 and Acts 15:35.

Barnabas did not withhold anything from God. As the hymn goes, *"Take my silver and my gold, not a mite will I withhold."* He actively participated in the ministry, not just giving his resources but offering himself for God's work. Beyond his generosity, Barnabas played a vital role in encouraging and mentoring others, especially Paul and John Mark. His encouragement and mentorship helped shape their ministries and further the spread of the gospel.

Beloved, how are you using the resources God has entrusted to you? Are you investing in the kingdom like Barnabas, or are you holding back? Are you actively involved in evangelism, teaching, or supporting others in their faith journey? Remember, the greatest legacy we can leave is not material wealth but lives transformed through our efforts.

Let us pray for the grace to follow Barnabas' example. Lord, take over our entire being and resources for Your kingdom's expansion. Help us to spend and be spent for Your glory. May we, like Barnabas, be generous, active, and faithful in spreading the gospel. Use us, Lord, to bring comfort and salvation to others. In Jesus Christ's mighty name, we pray. Amen.

God bless you as you commit to both giving and living for the Great Commission. Amen.

DAY 18

LUST OF THE EYES AND SPIRITUAL BLINDNESS

Job 31:1 *"I made a covenant with mine eyes; why then should I think upon a maid?"*

Judges 16:21 *"But the Philistines took him, and put out his eyes, and brought him down to Gaza, and bound him with fetters of brass; and he did grind in the prison house."*

Glory be to God in the Highest!

Beloved, today's devotional focuses on the profound connection between the eyes and the mind. Our eyes serve as gateways to the soul, influencing our thoughts and actions. There is a spiritual truth here that cannot be overstated: what we see often shapes what we desire. This is why Job's declaration of making a covenant with his eyes is so powerful. He understood that to control his thoughts and actions, he needed to guard what he allowed his eyes to see.

Consider Samson, a man chosen by God and gifted with extraordinary strength. Despite his divine calling, he fell prey to the lust of the eyes. His downfall began with what he saw, leading him to pursue relationships that ultimately led to his capture and blindness. The Philistines, after capturing Samson, immediately gouged out his eyes. This act was not just physical but symbolic of how sin blinds us spiritually, stripping us of our vision and purpose.

David, too, fell victim to this same trap. It was after he *saw* Bathsheba bathing that he was overcome with lust, leading to a series of tragic events. Similarly, Solomon, in his wisdom and later regret, warned of the dangers of lust and the entrapment of immoral desires. In *Proverbs 23:26-28*, he describes how a whore is a deep ditch, waiting to ensnare those who fall into temptation.

Sin begins with what we allow into our hearts through our eyes. The enemy understands this and often uses it as a strategic entry point. If we are not vigilant, the lust of the eyes can lead us into spiritual blindness, rendering us powerless and disconnected from God's purpose.

Beloved, what is the state of your spiritual sight today? Are you guarding your eyes and mind against the traps of lust and temptation? Genuine repentance is the only way to restore spiritual vision. No matter your position or status, there is a need for humility and a return to holiness.

Pray this prayer: Heavenly Father, I make a covenant today with my eyes to focus on Your Word and Your ways. Help me to reject the lust of the eyes and flesh, replacing it with agape love. Strengthen me to walk in purity and holiness. In Jesus Christ's mighty name, I pray. Amen.

Fix your gaze on Jesus, as Hebrews 12:2 admonishes: *"Looking unto Jesus, the author and finisher of our faith."* Make a covenant with your eyes today, choosing to focus on God's Word and His ways.

God bless you. Stay vigilant and guard your spiritual sight.

DAY 19

A STERN WARNING TO PASTORS (SHEPHARDS)

1 Corinthians 10:8 *"Neither let us commit fornication, as some of them committed, and fell in one day three and twenty thousand."*

1 Corinthians 10:11-12 *"Now all these things happened unto them for ensamples: and they are written for our admonition, upon whom the ends of the world are come. Wherefore let him that thinketh he standeth take heed lest he fall."*

Glory be to God in the Highest!

Today's devotional comes with a serious warning for ministers and shepherds in God's vineyard. Samson's tragic downfall serves as a timeless example of the devastating consequences of sexual sin. Though anointed and set apart as a Nazarite to deliver Israel, Samson fell victim to the sin of fornication. The result was a loss of his divine connection, blindness, captivity, and humiliation (Judges 16:21).

Sexual sin is one of the quickest ways to lose a ministry and divine calling. Ministers are prime targets of the enemy because of the influence they wield in the Kingdom of God. No one is immune, regardless of their level of anointing or spiritual stature. The Word of God admonishes us to **"take heed"** and be vigilant. Delilahs—both literal and symbolic—are always lurking, seeking to ensnare and derail God's servants.

To avoid such pitfalls, pastors and ministers must adopt several strategies:

1.) Flee from temptation: As Joseph fled from Potiphar's wife, we must not linger in compromising situations.

2.) Define relationships clearly: Boundaries should be set in all interactions to prevent any appearance of evil.

3.) Remain watchful and prayerful: Constant vigilance and reliance on the Holy Spirit are necessary to withstand the enemy's schemes.

4.) Never take God's grace for granted: The grace of God is not a license to sin. It empowers us to live holy lives.

A few years ago, I received a call from a woman requesting prayer at her home. Sensing the potential danger, I insisted that my wife accompany me. Upon arrival, the woman was dressed inappropriately, clearly attempting to seduce me. The presence of my wife thwarted the enemy's plan, and I thank God for delivering me from that trap.

The lesson here is clear: **Do not tempt God.** Taking unnecessary risks, like climbing a palm tree with a weak rope, is foolish and dangerous (Matthew 4:7). Avoiding temptation altogether is the safest course.

Confession and genuine repentance are crucial for any minister who has fallen into sin. Openly acknowledging sin before the congregation can bring healing and restoration. Above all, remain watchful and prayerful, keeping your body under the Holy Spirit's control.

Father, we receive grace to keep our bodies under the subjection of the Holy Spirit. Like Joseph, empower us to resist sin, even unto the shedding of blood. Keep us holy and blameless before You. In Jesus Christ's mighty name, we pray. Amen.

Take a moment to evaluate your life and ministry. Identify any areas where boundaries may be weak or compromised and work towards strengthening those weakness. Commit to spending time in prayer daily, asking God for grace to live a holy and blameless life.

God bless you. Stay vigilant and guard your calling!

DAY 20

FORNICATION – FINAL WARNING

1 Corinthians 10:8 *"Neither let us commit fornication, as some of them committed, and fell in one day three and twenty thousand."*

Numbers 25:1-3 *"And Israel abode in Shittim, and the people began to commit whoredom with the daughters of Moab. And they called the people unto the sacrifices of their gods: and the people did eat, and bowed down to their gods. And Israel joined himself unto Baalpeor: and the anger of the LORD was kindled against Israel."*

Glory be to God in the Highest! The kingdom of darkness rejoices when a child of God falls into fornication, knowing it can lead to spiritual ruin and even death. In today's reading, Balaam, having failed to curse Israel, devised a more insidious plan. Through fornication with the daughters of Moab, Israel was lured into idolatry, leading to God's judgment. As a result, 24,000 people perished in one day (Numbers 25:9).

Fornication and idolatry are often intertwined. Once physical purity is compromised, spiritual compromise often follows. Solomon, despite his wisdom, fell victim to this trap. His foreign wives turned his heart to other gods, leading him away from the Lord (1 Kings 11:4-5). Similarly, Samson, ordained as a deliverer, became a trophy in the temple of Dagon after succumbing to the lure of Delilah (Judges 16:23).

Satan uses fornication to gain access to believers' lives. Sexual sin creates spiritual openings for demonic influence. Paul warns in *1 Corinthians 6:18* to flee from fornication, emphasizing that it is a sin against one's own body, which is the temple of the Holy Spirit.

To Avoid Fornication: **1. Guard Your Eyes and Mind:** Avoid pornography and other immoral content. Fill your mind with God's Word and meditate on it daily. **2. Set Boundaries:** Establish clear limits in relationships and avoid compromising situations. **3. Watch and Pray:** Constant vigilance and prayer are essential to overcoming temptation. **4. Stay Spirit-Filled:** Be continually filled with the Holy Spirit, who empowers believers to live holy lives.

Father, we acknowledge the dangers of fornication and idolatry. Help us to remain pure, guarding our hearts and minds. Fill us daily with Your Spirit, empowering us to live in holiness. Keep us vigilant and steadfast in Your Word. In Jesus Christ's mighty name, we pray. Amen.

Reflect on areas in your life where boundaries may be weak. Make a covenant with your eyes and mind, as Job did

(Job 31:1), committing to purity. Write down a personal action plan to avoid temptation and stay accountable to someone trustworthy.

God bless you. Amen.

DAY 21

BE A VICTOR AND NOT A TERRORIST!

Romans 8:37 *"Nay, in all these things we are more than conquerors through him that loved us."*

Judges 16:29-30 *"And Samson took hold of the two middle pillars upon which the house stood, and on which it was borne up, of the one with his right hand, and of the other with his left. And Samson said, Let me die with the Philistines. And he bowed himself with all his might; and the house fell upon the lords, and upon all the people that were therein. So the dead which he slew at his death were more than they which he slew in his life."*

Glory be to God in the Highest!

Death is a certainty that no one can escape. Whether timely or untimely, natural or accidental, it marks the end of earthly existence. The inevitability of death should drive us to live in a state of readiness, working out our salvation with fear and trembling (Philippians 2:12). Samson's life is a solemn example of how unrestrained desires can lead to a tragic end.

Samson, once a mighty deliverer, fell into disgrace due to his entanglement with Delilah. His disobedience and moral failure led to his capture, the loss of his vision, and humiliation at the hands of the Philistines. In a final act of desperation, he prayed for strength and brought down the temple of Dagon, killing himself along with his enemies. Though he achieved a measure of victory in death, it was a hollow one. He died prematurely, unfulfilled, and without fully realizing his God-given potential.

The consequences of sin are severe, especially sins like fornication and adultery, which are like fire that consumes everything in its path. They bring regret, destroy lives, and allow the enemy to gain control. Samson's story reminds us that yielding to such sins can lead to spiritual blindness and loss of purpose. However, Joseph's example shows that victory is possible. In Potiphar's house, he fled from temptation, choosing integrity over momentary pleasure. His decision not only preserved his destiny but also honored God.

Finishing well requires vigilance and discipline. It is not enough to start the Christian race strong; we must endure to the end. Living a life of purpose, obedience, and holiness ensures that we leave this world as victors, not as victims of poor choices.

Let us pray: Father, we ask for the grace to live victoriously, avoiding the traps of fornication and adultery. Help us to keep our bodies and minds under subjection, living as temples of the Holy Spirit. May we finish our race with honor, bringing glory to Your name. In Jesus Christ's mighty name, we pray. Amen.

Examine your life today. Are there areas where you have compromised? Are you taking your salvation seriously? Resolve to avoid anything that could compromise your spiritual integrity. Pray for strength and grace to live a life pleasing to God, free from the chains of sin.

God bless you. Amen.

DAY 22

SALVATION: A MAJOR PURSUIT

Matthew 6:33 *"But seek ye first the kingdom of God, and his righteousness; and all these things shall be added unto you."*

Jude 1:3-4 *"Beloved, when I gave all diligence to write unto you of the common salvation, it was needful for me to write unto you, and exhort you that ye should earnestly contend for the faith which was once delivered unto the saints. For there are certain men crept in unawares, who were before of old ordained to this condemnation, ungodly men, turning the grace of our God into lasciviousness, and denying the only Lord God, and our Lord Jesus Christ."*

Glory be to God in the Highest! A critical question confronts us today: What are you living for? Many people live aimlessly, without understanding their divine purpose. They eat, drink, marry, and pursue earthly pleasures, but never pause to consider why they are here. Life without purpose is like chasing the wind, and unfortunately, few people seek answers to this fundamental question.

Nicodemus, a respected leader in his time, pondered this question and sought answers from Jesus (John 3). He wanted to know the path to God's kingdom. Jesus's response highlighted the necessity of being born again—a call to salvation and spiritual rebirth. Our primary pursuit in life should be securing a place in God's kingdom, not accumulating fleeting worldly pleasures.

Everything in this world is temporary. Wealth, fame, and possessions will pass away, but eternity is forever. Each of us is working toward an eternal destination: heaven or hell. Salvation is the key to heaven, and it must be our highest priority.

Are you truly saved? If so, guard your salvation with all diligence, knowing that distractions and temptations abound. If not, today is the day to repent and accept Jesus Christ as your Lord and Savior. Do not delay, for tomorrow is not promised.

Let us pray: Father, help us to seek Your kingdom above all else. Keep us focused on our salvation and strengthen us to guard it jealously. Grant us the grace to live purposefully and to finish our race with joy. In Jesus Christ's mighty name, we pray.

God bless you. Amen.

DAY 23

THE SOLID (στερεός, *stereos*) FOUNDATION

1 Corinthians 3:11 "For other foundation can no man lay than that is laid, which is Jesus Christ."

Luke 6:47-49 "Whosoever cometh to me, and heareth my sayings, and doeth them, I will shew you to whom he is like: He is like a man which built an house, and digged deep, and laid the foundation on a rock: and when the flood arose, the stream beat vehemently upon that house, and could not shake it: for it was founded upon a rock. But he that heareth, and doeth not, is like a man that without a foundation built an house upon the earth; against which the stream did beat vehemently, and immediately it fell; and the ruin of that house was great."

Glory be to God in the Highest!

A foundation, as defined in building terms, is the lowest, load-bearing part of a structure, often hidden but crucial. In spiritual terms, it represents the underlying principles upon which our faith and lives are built. The strength of any structure, whether physical or spiritual, is determined by its foundation. A weak foundation cannot withstand pressure, but a strong, solid foundation ensures stability and longevity.

In civil engineering, the foundation is designed to bear the load of the structure. It is often deeper and stronger than the visible parts of the building. Similarly, in life, what we build upon—our faith, values, and principles—determines how we withstand the storms of life.

God, the Master Builder, prioritizes foundations. In Psalms 104:5, we read, "*Who laid the foundations of the earth, that it should not be removed forever.*" A solid foundation is firm, stable, and enduring, even amidst turbulent waters (Psalms 104:3).

Jesus Christ is the ultimate foundation. When we build our lives on Him, as described in Luke 6:47-49, we can withstand any storm. The man who hears and obeys the Word is like one who builds on a rock, ensuring security. In contrast, neglecting God's Word is like building on sand, leading to inevitable collapse.

What kind of foundation are you building your life upon? Is it solid rock or sinking sand? Reflect on your faith and ensure it is deeply rooted in Christ.

Lord, let our foundation receive Your divine touch. Strengthen and solidify it in Jesus Christ's mighty name. Help us to build our lives on the solid rock of Your Word.

God bless you. Amen.

DAY 24

THE SOLID (στερεός, *stereos*) FOUNDATION II

2 Chronicles 8:16 *"Now all the work of Solomon was prepared unto the day of the foundation of the house of the LORD, and until it was finished. So the house of the LORD was perfected."*

1 Kings 7:9-10 *"All these were of costly stones, according to the measures of hewed stones, sawed with saws, within and without, even from the foundation unto the coping, and so on the outside toward the great court. And the foundation was of costly stones, even great stones, stones of ten cubits, and stones of eight cubits."*

Glory be to God in the Highest!

Yesterday, we explored the concept of a solid foundation, emphasizing its importance in spiritual matters. Today, we delve deeper into its physical and practical aspects to broaden our understanding. King Solomon, known for his wisdom, meticulously built not only the temple of God but also his palace and other structures during his reign.

In our Bible reading, we see that Solomon, as a wise master builder, prioritized the foundation of every structure. These foundations were made of costly, hewed stones, precisely cut and fitted. The materials were not ordinary; they were chiseled from igneous rock—durable and enduring. Despite centuries of turmoil in the Middle East, these hidden foundations remain intact, a testament to their strength and quality.

Foundations are critical in every aspect of life, not just in buildings. They determine the stability and longevity of what is built upon them. Whether it is a marriage, faith, family, or any relationship, the nature of the foundation is what sustains it through challenges. Solomon's use of stones measuring ten by eight cubits highlights the deliberate effort to ensure durability and stability.

Many people only see what is above ground, but the true strength of any structure lies in its foundation. This principle applies to our spiritual lives, careers, and relationships. A weak foundation leads to collapse, but a solid one ensures endurance.

Take time today to examine the foundations in your life. Are they built on the solid rock of Christ, or are they on shaky ground? Ask God to reveal areas that need reinforcement and to help you build on the unshakable foundation of His Word.

Open our eyes, Lord, to discern the nature of our foundation. Strengthen and secure every aspect of our lives in Jesus Christ's mighty name. God bless you. Amen!

DAY 25

A FAULTY (ἐλαττωματικός, *Elattomatikos*) FOUNDATION

Galatians 6:7 "Be not deceived; God is not mocked: for whatsoever a man soweth, that shall he also reap."

Genesis 19:36-38 "Thus were both the daughters of Lot with child by their father. And the firstborn bare a son, and called his name Moab: the same is the father of the Moabites unto this day. And the younger, she also bare a son, and called his name Benammi: the same is the father of the children of Ammon unto this day."

Glory be to God in the Highest!

After reflecting on the importance of a solid foundation, today we turn our attention to the dangers of a faulty one. A faulty foundation, by definition, is imperfect, deficient, or defective. Its flaws may not be immediately visible but can cause significant damage over time. Like structural weaknesses in a building, faulty foundations in life are often hidden and require deep examination.

The story of Lot and his daughters provides a powerful example. After the destruction of Sodom and Gomorrah, Lot and his daughters found themselves isolated and faithless. Instead of trusting God for deliverance, they took matters into their own hands. Lot, weakened by drunkenness, and his daughters, influenced by their upbringing in a corrupt society, committed the grave sin of incest. This act laid a deeply flawed foundation, resulting in the birth of Moab and Ammon, whose descendants became perpetual enemies of Israel.

This story highlights the long-lasting consequences of faulty foundations. Just as a weak root system affects the health of a tree, poor decisions and sinful actions today shape future outcomes. The Moabites and Ammonites faced judgment for generations because of the foundation their ancestors laid.

In today's world, many lives, families, and institutions are built on faulty foundations. If we do not address these underlying issues, they can lead to collapse. Examine your own foundation: What seeds have you sown? What roots are you nurturing? If there are faults, only God's mercy can repair and restore.

Take time to reflect and allow the Holy Spirit to reveal any hidden flaws. Repent of past mistakes and seek God's intervention. Remember, God is not mocked; every action has consequences. But through His grace, faulty foundations can be made strong again.

Lord, We ask for Your mercy to heal and restore every faulty foundation in our lives. Help us to sow good seeds and build on the solid rock of Christ. In Jesus' mighty name.

God bless you. Amen!

DAY 26

FAITH AS A FOUNDATION

1 Timothy 6:19 *"Laying up in store for themselves a good foundation against the time to come, that they may lay hold on eternal life."*

Hebrews 11:8-10 *"By faith Abraham, when he was called to go out into a place which he should after receive for an inheritance, obeyed; and he went out, not knowing whither he went. By faith he sojourned in the land of promise, as in a strange country, dwelling in tabernacles with Isaac and Jacob, the heirs with him of the same promise: For he looked for a city which hath foundations, whose builder and maker is God."*

Glory be to God in the Highest! Foundation is the corner-stone of everything in life. It determines stability, longevity, and ultimate success. Without a proper foundation, no structure can stand. Spiritually, faith is the foundational element upon which our relationship with God and eternal destiny rest.

The story of Abraham exemplifies this truth. At the age of 75, Abraham made a life-changing decision based on faith alone. He left behind the familiar comforts of Padanaram, his birthplace, and the idolatry of his father's house. In obedience to God's call, he embarked on a journey to an unknown land, enduring hardship and uncertainty. His focus was not on earthly comforts but on the promise of an eternal city, a place whose foundation is laid by God Himself.

Despite living in tents alongside Isaac and Jacob, Abraham's faith never wavered. He saw beyond the temporary and trusted in God's eternal plan. His contemporaries may have mocked him, calling him foolish for leaving behind wealth and security. Yet, Abraham understood that faith builds a structure that lasts forever. His journey from Haran to Canaan, though challenging, laid a foundation for generations to come.

This eternal city, whose builder is God, represents heaven—a place we must prepare for while on earth. Abraham's faith became the blueprint for all believers, teaching us that true foundations are not built on visible things but on the unseen and eternal.

Jesus, in His conversation with Nicodemus in John 3, emphasized the need for a solid spiritual foundation: being born again. Just as Abraham left Haran, we must leave behind sin, idolatry, and worldly attachments to build on the foundation of faith in Christ.

Have you truly left behind your "Haran", the place of sin and idolatry? Is your foundation built on faith in God or on worldly things?

Lord, help us to lay a strong foundation of faith, trusting in Your promises and seeking the eternal city. Strengthen our resolve to leave behind all that hinders my walk with You. In Jesus' mighty name.

God bless you. Amen!

DAY 27

FOUNDATION AS A ROOT (Quid est stare in aliqua)

Romans 11:22 *"Behold therefore the goodness and severity of God: on them which fell, severity; but toward thee, goodness, if thou continue in his goodness: otherwise thou also shalt be cut off."*

Romans 11:16-18 *"For if the firstfruit be holy, the lump is also holy: and if the root be holy, so are the branches. And if some of the branches be broken off, and thou, being a wild olive tree, wert graffed in among them, and with them partakest of the root and fatness of the olive tree; Boast not against the branches. But if thou boast, thou bearest not the root, but the root thee."*

Glory be to God in the Highest!

Foundation can be likened to a root, which is the source of life and sustenance for any structure or being. Just as no tree can thrive without its root, no life can flourish without a solid foundation. In the context of faith, our spiritual root is critical—it determines the strength, growth, and endurance of our walk with God.

The analogy of the root in Romans 11 teaches that the holiness of the root affects the entire tree. If the root is holy, the branches will also be holy. The same principle applies to our spiritual lives. A faulty or non-existent foundation leads to instability. This is why the root of our faith is essential; it shapes the kind of life we live and the legacy we leave.

Apostle Paul warns against boasting about being grafted into the faith. The root, not the branches, carries and nourishes. In the same way, our spiritual growth and sustenance come from being deeply rooted in Christ.

In Yoruba philosophy, a common saying emphasizes that a river that forgets its source will dry up. This truth resonates with the biblical teaching that a life disconnected from its spiritual root will wither. Many issues within the church today stem from weak or non-existent foundations. A solid spiritual root requires proper discipleship, mentorship, and grounding in the Word of God.

Reflect on your spiritual journey. Who laid your foundation? Were you properly discipled? Have you maintained a connection to your spiritual source? Your faith must be rooted in Christ, nurtured through sound teaching and consistent fellowship with God.

Ask God to purify your spiritual root and strengthen your foundation in Christ.

Pray for Nigeria, asking God to heal the nation's foundation and restore righteousness.

Commit to deepening your connection to God, seeking His guidance and nourishment daily.

May God help us to stand firm, deeply rooted in His Word, bearing fruits that glorify His name.

God bless You. Amen!

DAY 28

FOUNDATION POWERS

1 Kings 16:34 "In his days did Hiel the Bethelite build Jericho: he laid the foundation thereof in Abiram his firstborn, and set up the gates thereof in his youngest son Segub, according to the word of the LORD, which he spake by Joshua the son of Nun."

Joshua 6:26 "And Joshua adjured them at that time, saying, Cursed be the man before the LORD, that riseth up and buildeth this city Jericho: he shall lay the foundation thereof in his firstborn, and in his youngest son shall he set up the gates of it."

Glory be to God in the Highest! Power is the force behind every action and movement. In the spiritual sense, power influences foundational matters, determining the success or failure of what is built upon it. Foundations are never neutral; they are either empowered by divine or demonic forces. The story of Jericho's rebuilding in our Bible reading today demonstrates how spiritual pronouncements can shape the destiny of a place or person.

Joshua's curse upon anyone who would rebuild Jericho was not mere words but carried divine power. Hiel the Bethelite, ignoring this curse, embarked on the project and suffered the loss of his two sons—his firstborn, Abiram, when laying the foundation, and his youngest, Segub, when setting up the gates. This tragedy underscores the power of foundational pronouncements.

Many struggles today have their roots in foundational issues. Curses, covenants, or sinful deeds of the past often manifest as barrenness, untimely death, poverty, or other afflictions. Just as Elisha reversed the curse on Jericho's water through divine intervention, we must rely on the power of Jesus Christ's blood to address and neutralize any negative foundational powers at work in our lives.

The blood of Jesus has the power to cleanse, break curses, and establish new, godly foundations. We must trust in this divine power to reverse every negative effect of past foundations and to build our lives on the solid rock of Christ.

Ask God to reveal and rectify every faulty foundation in your life.

Pray that the power in the blood of Jesus will break all negative pronouncements affecting your destiny.

Declare that your life, family, and future are built on the solid foundation of Jesus Christ.

God bless you. Amen.

DAY 29

FOUNDATION POWERS II

Numbers 20:12 "And the LORD spake unto Moses and Aaron, Because ye believed me not, to sanctify me in the eyes of the children of Israel, therefore ye shall not bring this congregation into the land which I have given them."

Genesis 49:5-7 "Simeon and Levi are brethren; instruments of cruelty are in their habitations.

O my soul, come not thou into their secret; unto their assembly, mine honour, be not thou united: for in their anger they slew a man, and in their selfwill they digged down a wall.

Cursed be their anger, for it was fierce; and their wrath, for it was cruel: I will divide them in Jacob, and scatter them in Israel."

Glory be to God in the Highest! Moses, the great servant of God, performed remarkable feats by divine power. He led the Israelites out of Egypt, communed directly with God, and wielded miraculous authority. Yet, despite his spiritual stature, Moses fell victim to a foundational curse tied to his genealogy. His parents were Levites, and the curse pronounced by Jacob upon Levi in Genesis 49 became a ticking time bomb in Moses' life.

This foundational power manifested at Kadesh, where Moses, in a moment of anger, struck the rock instead of speaking to it as God commanded. This act of disobedience barred him from entering the Promised Land. This is the power of foundational curses.

Like Moses, many today carry the weight of unaddressed foundational issues, often unaware of their roots. These curses, spoken over generations, silently wait for moments of vulnerability to manifest. This is why understanding and addressing our genealogical roots is essential. Foundational powers respect no one, regardless of spiritual position or achievements.

Beloved, it is crucial to prayerfully address these foundational issues. Research your family history, particularly through cultural panegyrics if available, and seek divine intervention. Through the power of the blood of Jesus, these foundational powers can be broken. Christ has redeemed us from the curse of the law (Galatians 3:13-14).

Ask God to reveal any hidden foundational issues affecting your life.

Plead the blood of Jesus over your foundation and break every generational curse.

I Pray that God would grant us wisdom and strength to live

righteously and lay a godly foundation for future generations.

God bless you. Amen.

DAY 30

ADDRESSING FOUNDATIONAL ISSUES

2 Kings 2:22 *"So the waters have been healed to this day, according to the word spoken by Elisha."*

2 Kings 2:18-21 *"And when they came again to him, (for he tarried at Jericho,) he said unto them, Did I not say unto you, Go not?*

And the men of the city said unto Elisha, Behold, I pray thee, the situation of this city is pleasant, as my lord seeth: but the water is naught, and the ground barren.

And he said, Bring me a new cruse, and put salt therein. And they brought it to him.

And he went forth unto the spring of the waters, and cast the salt in there, and said, Thus saith the LORD, I have healed these waters; there shall not be from thence any more death or barren land."

Glory be to God in the highest! The curse pronounced by Joshua over Jericho (Joshua 6:26) did not just affect the physical structure of the city but also poisoned its water supply and made its land barren. When Hiel rebuilt Jericho's walls (1 Kings 16:34), the curse remained because only an anointed servant of God could reverse it.

Water, a symbol of life, had become bitter and useless. The land itself was barren, rendering all efforts fruitless. This paints a vivid picture: no matter how skilled or educated someone may be—whether trained at Harvard or the London School of Economics—when a foundation is cursed, human efforts will ultimately fail.

This is the reality for many nations, communities, and families today. There are foundational issues—spiritual and generational—that hinder progress and prosperity. However, just as Elisha, led by the Spirit of God, addressed the root of Jericho's problem, we too must confront these issues head-on.

Elisha's actions were symbolic but powerful. By adding salt to the spring and making a prophetic declaration, he brought healing to the waters and the land. This act reminds us that God can heal and restore any broken foundation. No more death. No more barrenness.

It's important to examine our family history and spiritual foundations. Patterns of failure, hardship, or stagnation may indicate deeper issues that need God's healing touch. Take time to seek God's guidance and pray for the restoration of your family and lineage.

Lord, We invite You into the foundation of our lives and family. Heal every broken place and reverse every curse that hinders progress. Restore life, fruitfulness, and prosperity to our households. In Jesus' name, Amen.

God is the ultimate healer of foundations. Trust Him to restore what has been lost and make every bitter situation sweet again.

God bless you. Amen.

DAY 31

COURTSHIP – THE FOUNDATION OF MARRIAGE (PART 1)

Hebrews 13:4 "*Marriage is honourable in all, and the bed undefiled: but whoremongers and adulterers God will judge.*"

Matthew 19:4-6 "*And he answered and said unto them, Have ye not read, that he which made them at the beginning made them male and female, And said, For this cause shall a man leave father and mother, and shall cleave to his wife: and they twain shall be one flesh? Wherefore they are no more twain, but one flesh. What therefore God hath joined together, let not man put asunder.*"

Glory be to God in the highest! Marriage is a sacred union designed by God. In today's Bible reading, Jesus quotes Genesis 2:24, emphasizing that marriage is a binding, life-long covenant between a man and a woman. Just as metals are combined to form a stronger alloy, marriage brings two individuals together to form something greater. However, the strength of this union depends on its foundation—and that foundation is courtship.

A home, which forms the basic unit of society, is established through marriage. When the foundation of marriage is faulty, the home is at risk. Unfortunately, many Christian marriages today are built on shaky foundations, often due to hasty or unwise courtship decisions. A house built on falsehood cannot stand; it's only a matter of time before it collapses.

Marriage is honorable and desirable for mature believers. But getting it right from the start is crucial. Proverbs 18:22 reminds us, *"Whoso findeth a wife findeth a good thing, and obtaineth favour of the LORD."* This applies equally to those seeking husbands. However, it's important to distinguish between a spouse chosen according to God's will and one chosen based on worldly criteria.

A Christ-centered foundation is essential for any marriage that will endure. Beyond spiritual compatibility, it's also important to consider other factors such as **Medical Compatibility**; Understanding each other's genotype and health status and **Academic and Career Goals:** Aligning future plans and aspirations.

Church leaders should prioritize marriage seminars and counseling to equip singles and couples with biblical wisdom. These teachings can help address and repair any faulty foundations.

Pray this Prayer: *Lord, I commit my relationships into Your hands. Help me to build on the solid foundation of Christ.*

For those whose marriages are struggling due to faulty foundations, I pray for Your divine intervention and restoration. In Jesus' name, Amen. A strong marriage begins with a strong foundation. Ensure Christ is at the center of your courtship and future home.

God bless you. Amen.

DAY 32

COURTSHIP – THE FOUNDATION OF MARRIAGE (PART 2)

Proverbs 18:22 *"Whoso findeth a wife findeth a good thing, and obtaineth favour of the LORD."*

Luke 1:26-28 *"And in the sixth month the angel Gabriel was sent from God unto a city of Galilee, named Nazareth,To a virgin espoused to a man whose name was Joseph, of the house of David; and the virgin's name was Mary. And the angel came in unto her, and said, Hail, thou that art highly favoured, the Lord is with thee: blessed art thou among women."*

Glory be to God in the highest! Mary, the mother of Jesus, was engaged to Joseph, and their courtship was built on holiness, purity, truthfulness, and integrity. They upheld the principle found in Hebrews 13:4: *"Marriage is honourable in all, and the bed undefiled: but whoremongers and adulterers God will judge."* Because they kept their relationship pure, God's favor rested upon them.

Mary's purity aligned her with the prophecy in Isaiah 7:14:*"Behold, a virgin shall conceive and bear a son, and shall call his name Immanuel."* Her decision to remain pure allowed her to play a key role in God's redemptive plan.

What an honorable foundation to build a marriage upon!

I recall a time when I asked an intending couple during a testimony service how they maintained their holiness throughout their courtship. My intent was to inspire the youth in the congregation, but the reaction was unexpected. The senior priest rebuked me because, unbeknownst to me, the couple was already four months pregnant. I felt deeply disheartened. However, this experience reinforced the importance of teaching and upholding godly standards in courtship.

Despite societal pressures, many believers still honor God by remaining pure until marriage. Each time a testimony of purity is shared, heaven rejoices. A solid foundation of holiness in courtship ensures a marriage that can withstand the challenges of life. Mary resisted temptation, and God honored her faithfulness by making her the mother of our Savior.

As a generation of believers, we must not remain silent. Through the power of the Holy Spirit, we have a responsibility to guide, counsel, and mentor the next generation. Our input can help them make godly decisions that honor Christ.

Lord, I pray for the younger generation, that You would preserve and guide them in their relationships. Help them to build on the solid foundation of purity and holiness. May they receive Your favor and walk in Your will. In Jesus' mighty name, Amen.

A foundation built on holiness and obedience to God will always stand strong. Trust God and honor Him in your relationships.

God bless you. Amen.

DAY 33

A SOLID MARITAL FOUNDATION – ISAAC AS A CASE STUDY

Genesis 24:67 *"And Isaac brought her into his mother Sarah's tent, and took Rebekah, and she became his wife; and he loved her: and Isaac was comforted after his mother's death."*

Genesis 24:37-40 *"And my master made me swear, saying, Thou shalt not take a wife to my son of the daughters of the Canaanites, in whose land I dwell:*

But thou shalt go unto my father's house, and to my kindred, and take a wife unto my son.

And I said unto my master, Peradventure the woman will not follow me.

And he said unto me, The LORD, before whom I walk, will send his angel with thee, and prosper thy way; and thou shalt take a wife for my son of my kindred, and of my father's house."

Glory be to God in the highest! The story of Isaac and Rebekah in Genesis 24 is one of the most inspiring examples of a godly marriage foundation. Abraham, understanding the importance of marriage in fulfilling God's covenant, took great care in ensuring that Isaac's spouse came from his own people—those aligned with God's purposes.

Abraham rejected the idea of Isaac marrying a Canaanite woman, despite their beauty, because he knew they were not suitable for a covenant relationship. In the same way, we must prioritize spiritual alignment over outward appearances when seeking life partners. A kingdom-minded marriage requires a foundation built on shared faith and values.

Abraham's servant, Eliezer, embarked on this journey prayerfully, trusting that God would lead him to the right person. God answered by bringing Rebekah into Isaac's life. Rebekah's qualities stood out: **Maturity and Readiness;** Rebekah was of marriageable age and capable of making her own decisions, **Kindness and Servanthood;** She willingly provided water for Eliezer and all his camels, demonstrating a heart of service (Genesis 24:19-20) and **Purity;** Rebekah was a virgin, preserving herself for marriage. God honored this purity by making her the mother of Israel.

Even when Isaac and Rebekah faced challenges, such as delayed conception, their foundation in God sustained them.

In the early 1990s, my close friend, David Olalekan (a missionary with RCCG), and I made a commitment to marry daughters of Zion—women rooted in Christ. Today, we are both grateful for the decision to prioritize godly principles in our marriages.

Parents should actively guide their children in making godly marital choices, just as Abraham did. Prayer and reliance on the Holy Spirit—the ultimate matchmaker—are essential. As 2 Corinthians 6:14 reminds us, we should not be unequally yoked with unbelievers.

Lord, I pray for all singles seeking life partners. Guide them to make the right choices, and may their marriages be built on the solid foundation of Christ. Bless our families and lead our children in Your ways. In Jesus' name, Amen.

A godly marriage foundation begins with prayer, purity, and the leading of the Holy Spirit. Trust God's timing and guidance in all things.

God bless you. Amen.

DAY 34

PARENTAL GUIDANCE – A KEY TO A STRONG MARITAL FOUNDATION

Psalms 11:3 *"If the foundations be destroyed, what can the righteous do?"*

Genesis 26:34-35 *"And Esau was forty years old when he took to wife Judith the daughter of Beeri the Hittite, and Bashemath the daughter of Elon the Hittite:*

Which were a grief of mind unto Isaac and to Rebekah."

Glory be to God in the highest! Continuing our focus on marital foundations, today we examine the cautionary tale of Esau's marriage. After selling his birthright, Esau compounded his mistakes by marrying women from the Hittites—a decision that brought sorrow to his parents, Isaac and Rebekah. Unlike his father and grandfather, Esau ignored the pattern of seeking parental guidance and married women who were culturally and spiritually incompatible with the family's covenant purpose.

Jacob, on the other hand, followed the family tradition. He sought his parents' counsel and went to his grandfather's homeland to find a suitable wife. This demonstrates the value of involving parents in marital decisions. While modern society emphasizes personal choice, the wisdom and experience of godly parents—both biological and spiritual—remain vital in laying a solid marital foundation.

In one of the assemblies I pastored, a couple with a shaky marital foundation constantly caused turmoil. Their relationship was marked by infidelity and substance abuse. My wife and I were frequently called to intervene, even late at night, and once had to mediate at a police station. Their lack of a godly foundation made reconciliation difficult, but by God's grace, progress was made. This experience underscored the truth of Psalm 11:3: *"If the foundations be destroyed, what can the righteous do?"* A faulty foundation makes stability nearly impossible, but God's mercy can still intervene and bring restoration.

Esau's decision to marry outside God's will hindered the fulfillment of God's promises through him. Parents, take note: allowing your children to make unguided marital decisions can lead to lasting grief. Just as Isaac and Rebekah suffered, parents today must be vigilant and involved in their children's choices.

In this "jet age," young people often dismiss the wisdom of the "old school." However, seeking counsel from parents and spiritual mentors is crucial. Proverbs 11:14 reminds us that *"in the multitude of counselors there is safety."* A godly marriage foundation begins with prayer, guidance, and obedience to God's principles.

Parents, be proactive. Offer guidance and counsel rooted in love and godly wisdom. Young people, seek input from those who care for you spiritually and emotionally. Build your marital foundation on Christ, ensuring it will stand the test of time.

Lord, I pray for every home struggling with foundational issues. Bring healing, restoration, and guidance. Help parents to be vigilant and young people to seek Your will in their choices. May our homes be built on the solid rock of Christ. In Jesus' name, Amen.

A godly foundation is necessary for a thriving marriage. Seek wisdom, involve parents, and trust God's leading.

God bless you. Amen.

DAY 35

THE EFFECTS OF A FAULTY FOUNDATION IN MARRIAGE

Matthew 7:27 *"And the rain descended, and the floods came, and the winds blew, and beat upon that house; and it fell: and great was the fall of it."*

Job 22:15-16 *"Hast thou marked the old way which wicked men have trodden?*

Which were cut down out of time, whose foundation was overflown with a flood."

Glory be to God in the Highest! Beloved, welcome to another time of refreshing in God's Word. Today, we continue exploring the importance of a solid foundation in marriage. A strong foundation is not just a starting point—it is the bedrock that determines whether a marriage can withstand life's inevitable storms.

Prevention is always better than cure. Just as a physical structure requires regular maintenance, a marriage, no matter how well-founded, needs ongoing care. Wise builders know to lay a foundation on rock—something solid, stable, and immovable. Spiritually, that Rock is none other than Jesus Christ, the cornerstone on which every godly marriage must be built.

Storms in life are not a question of *if* but *when*. Whether they come in the early, middle, or latter years, they are inevitable. These storms—financial struggles, health challenges, misunderstandings, or external pressures—test the strength of a marriage. As our memory verse reminds us, rain will fall, floods will rise, and winds will blow. The key question is: *What is your foundation?*

The story of the Shunammite woman in 2 Kings 4:8-37 teaches us that faith and preparation are essential. She declared, "It is well," not because everything was perfect, but because she trusted in God's sovereignty.

About fourteen years ago, my wife, Taiwo, and I faced a storm that shook us to our core. It was a dreadful, life-threatening experience that tested our faith. I vividly recall those days at Prayer City, along the Lagos-Ibadan Expressway in Nigeria. The situation seemed hopeless, and fear gripped my heart. Yet, because of the solid foundation we had laid during seven years of holy courtship, we were able to stand firm.

Through God's mercy, we overcame. If not for that foundation in Christ, our story might have ended differently. Indeed, Jesus proved to be our *shelter in the time of storm*, and for that, we give Him eternal praise.

Jesus Christ is the *Rock of Ages*, the only sure foundation. A marriage built on anything else—whether wealth, beauty, or worldly wisdom—cannot withstand life's storms. But when Christ is at the center, the marriage will endure.

Ensure your marriage is built on the unshakable foundation of Christ. Maintain your foundation through regular prayer, communication, and godly counsel help maintain a strong marriage. Expect and Prepare for Storms because Trials will come, but with Christ as your anchor, you will over-come.

Lord Jesus, You are the solid rock upon which we build our lives and marriages. Help us never to compromise in setting our foundations on You. Strengthen every marriage that is struggling today, and be the shelter in every storm. In Your mighty name, we pray. Amen.

A marriage founded on Christ can withstand any storm. Trust Him to be your shelter and strength.

God bless you. Amen.

DAY 36

THE ETERNAL ROCK OF AGES

Psalms 62:7 "*In God is my salvation and my glory: the rock of my strength, and my refuge, is in God.*"

Matthew 7:24-27 "*Therefore whosoever heareth these sayings of mine, and doeth them, I will liken him unto a wise man, which built his house upon a rock:*

And the rain descended, and the floods came, and the winds blew, and beat upon that house; and it fell not: for it was founded upon a rock.

And every one that heareth these sayings of mine, and doeth them not, shall be likened unto a foolish man, which built his house upon the sand:

And the rain descended, and the floods came, and the winds blew, and beat upon that house; and it fell: and great was the fall of it."

Glory be to God in the Highest! When it comes to foundations—whether in faith, marriage, or any aspect of life—the strength and stability of the foundation determine the resilience of the structure. A wise builder knows the importance of setting a firm, reliable base. Spiritually, the only true foundation is *Christ Jesus*, the **Eternal Rock of Ages**.

The size and weight of a structure demand a foundation that can sustain it. Likewise, the greater your purpose or calling, the stronger your foundation must be in Christ. Jesus is not just any rock—He is the Rock that is immovable, unbreakable, and eternal. Only He can uphold anything built on Him.

In Daniel 2:35, the vision of King Nebuchadnezzar reveals a divine Rock cut without human hands. This Rock destroyed the image of worldly powers, symbolizing Christ's unshakable kingdom. The world may offer various foundations—wealth, status, or human wisdom—but all are like sinking sand. Only Christ can fill the entire earth and endure forever.

A house built on sand will collapse under pressure. In contrast, a life built on Christ will withstand the storms of life. Jesus likens those who obey His words to wise builders. Obedience strengthens your spiritual foundation. When life's trials come, those rooted in Christ remain immovable, undeterred by challenges.

Jesus declared in Matthew 16:18 that He would build His Church on the confession that He is the Messiah. This foundation ensures that no matter how fiercely the gates of hell attack, they will not prevail. Believers who stand on this truth become part of an unshakable kingdom.

"All other ground is sinking sand." Dig deep and build on

the Eternal Rock. Let Christ be your shelter, fortress, and refuge.

Pray this Prayer: *Lord Jesus, You are the Eternal Rock of Ages. I rededicate my life to You today. Be my firm foundation, my mighty fortress, and my refuge in every area of my life. Help me to build on You and stand firm through every trial. In Jesus' name, Amen.*

A life built on Christ is immovable, unshakable, and secure. Stand on the Rock that never fails.

God bless you. Amen.

DAY 37

THE FOUNDATION AND IT'S SEAL

2 Timothy 2:19 *"Nevertheless the foundation of God standeth sure, having this seal, The Lord knoweth them that are his. And, Let every one that nameth the name of Christ depart from iniquity."*

1 Corinthians 3:11-15 *"For other foundation can no man lay than that is laid, which is Jesus Christ. Now if any man build upon this foundation gold, silver, precious stones, wood, hay, stubble; Every man's work shall be made manifest: for the day shall declare it, because it shall be revealed by fire; and the fire shall try every man's work of what sort it is. If any man's work abide which he hath built thereupon, he shall receive a reward. If any man's work shall be burned, he shall suffer loss: but he himself shall be saved; yet so as by fire."*

Glory be to God in the Highest! Today's teaching emphasizes the importance of building rightly on a sure foundation. While the foundation—*Jesus Christ*—is perfect and unshakable, what we build on it matters greatly. The Apostle Paul warns that the quality of our work will be tested by fire.

The foundation of God stands **sure** and is sealed with a divine stamp of authenticity. This seal assures two key truths: 1. **God Knows His Own:** No one can deceive God. He knows those who genuinely belong to Him. 2. **Call to Holiness:** Those who bear the name of Christ must depart from iniquity. The seal requires that our lives reflect the purity and holiness of Christ.

Paul uses six materials to illustrate how we build on the foundation:

Gold, Silver, Precious Stones: These represent works done in obedience, faith, and love. They are enduring and fire-resistant.

Wood, Hay, Stubble: These represent works done with wrong motives, carelessness, or superficiality. They are combustible and will not survive the test.

Each person's work will be tested by fire. The question is: *Are you building with lasting materials?*

The Word of God is a mirror that reveals the true state of our hearts. It is critical to examine ourselves honestly and align our lives with His truth. Deception—especially self-deception—can lead to disastrous results. No position, title, or outward appearance can replace genuine faithfulness and obedience to God.

Lord, I thank You for the sure foundation of Christ. Help me to build my life with materials that will endure the test of time and fire. Deliver me from self-deception and guide me to live in holiness and truth. May my works bring glory to Your name. In Jesus' name, Amen.

Your foundation in Christ is sure—build wisely and with lasting, fire-resistant materials. Let your life reflect the holiness and truth of God's seal.

God bless you. Amen.

DAY 38

YOU ARE A CO-LABOURER

1 Corinthians 3:9 "For we are labourers together with God: ye are God's husbandry, ye are God's building."

1 Corinthians 3:9-10 "For we are labourers together with God: ye are God's husbandry, ye are God's building. According to the grace of God which is given unto me, as a wise masterbuilder, I have laid the foundation, and another buildeth thereon. But let every man take heed how he buildeth thereupon."

Glory be to God in the Highest! It is a profound privilege to be called a co-labourer with God. While the foundation of our spiritual lives is laid by Jesus Christ, the responsibility to build upon that foundation rests on us. God has given each of us the task of cultivating and constructing our spiritual lives as His temple and field. This partnership with God means that we are not passive observers but active participants in the work of our faith.

The foundation is already set on Christ, but how we build on it matters significantly. Paul reminds us in today's reading that there are different materials one can use: gold, silver, and precious stones, which represent faith, obedience, and works inspired by the Holy Spirit, or wood, hay, and stubble, which signify worldly pursuits and shallow commitments. The quality of our spiritual edifice will be tested by fire, and only what is built with enduring materials will last.

God expects us to continually build ourselves up in faith. Jude 1:20 emphasizes the importance of praying in the Holy Spirit, which strengthens and fortifies our foundation. Prayer, study of the Word, and a life of obedience are essential tools for constructing a lasting spiritual house. The onus is on each believer to take this responsibility seriously.

Being a co-labourer with God also means avoiding distractions. Like Martha, many of us are consumed by activities that, although good, do not contribute to our spiritual growth. It is easy to mistake busyness for productivity. However, the true measure of our work will be revealed when it is tested. Therefore, it is crucial to focus on what truly matters—our personal relationship with God.

As you reflect today, examine the materials you are using to build your life. Are they fireproof? Are you investing in your spiritual growth with prayer, the Word of God, and a heart aligned with His will? The day of testing will come, and only what is built with enduring materials will stand.

Lord Jesus, thank You for the privilege of partnering with You. Help me to build my life on a solid foundation, using materials that will endure. Strengthen my faith and remove every form of laziness and distraction. Guide me to grow deeper in prayer, study, and obedience, so that my life may glorify You. Amen.

As a co-labourer with God, take heed to build wisely. What you construct today will determine your spiritual resilience tomorrow.

God bless you. Amen.

DAY 39

DO NOT COMPROMISE — BUILD WITH GOD

Philippians 2:12 *"Wherefore, my beloved, as ye have always obeyed, not as in my presence only, but now much more in my absence, work out your own salvation with fear and trembling."*

Jude 1:20-23 *"But ye, beloved, building up yourselves on your most holy faith, praying in the Holy Ghost, keep yourselves in the love of God, looking for the mercy of our Lord Jesus Christ unto eternal life. And of some have compassion, making a difference: and others save with fear, pulling them out of the fire; hating even the garment spotted by the flesh."*

Glory be to God in the Highest! Today's devotional reminds us of the dangers of compromise, especially when it comes to building our spiritual lives. Having a blueprint or a good foundation is not enough if compromises are made in the actual building process. In God's dictionary, compromise does not exist. His principles are unchanging and His standards remain firm. As Paul admonishes, we must work out our salvation with "fear and trembling," maintaining reverence and seriousness in our walk with Him.

Compromise weakens the foundation and structure of any life. Abraham, despite being a man of faith, compromised by having a child with Hagar, leading to generational conflict. Demas, a once-faithful companion of Paul, compromised by loving the world, and he lost his place in the ministry. Ananias and Sapphira compromised their integrity and faced immediate judgment. These examples serve as sobering warnings: God's grace should never be taken for granted.

Building with gold, as mentioned in previous devotionals, refers to using materials that are pure, durable, and able to withstand the test of time and fire. In spiritual terms, this means living a life of holiness, obedience, and faithfulness. Prayer, studying God's Word, and loving others as Christ loves us are essential components of this process.

Today's reflection calls for a deep, honest examination of your heart. Are there areas where you have compromised? Perhaps in your faith, relationships, or moral convictions? God does not overlook compromise, and neither should we. Repentance is key. God is merciful and ready to restore those who turn to Him sincerely.

Pray this Prayer: *Father, forgive me for any areas in my life where I have compromised Your standards. Help me to build my life with gold—pure and holy materials that honor You. Restore me to a place of obedience and steadfastness.*

Strengthen me to walk in Your ways, and may I never take Your grace for granted. In Jesus' name, Amen.

May God bless you as you remain steadfast, refusing to compromise, and building with materials that will stand the test of time.

DAY 40

INCESSANT SPIRITUAL BUILDING COL-LAPSE

Galatians 2:18 *"For if I build again the things which I destroyed, I make myself a transgressor."*

Galatians 1:8-10 *"But though we, or an angel from heaven, preach any other gospel unto you than that which we have preached unto you, let him be accursed. As we said before, so say I now again, If any man preach any other gospel unto you than that ye have received, let him be accursed. For do I now persuade men, or God? or do I seek to please men? for if I yet pleased men, I should not be the servant of Christ."*

Glory be to God in the Highest! Today's message addresses a critical issue: the continuous collapse of spiritual edifices in the lives of individuals and congregations. Just as physical buildings crumble due to weak foundations, poor materials, or neglect, so too do spiritual lives falter when compromised by sin. The phenomenon of spiritual decline, or falling away from the faith, is alarmingly frequent in our time.

Abraham's compromise with Hagar, despite his solid foundation of faith, led to generational conflict and unrest. Likewise, compromise in any area of life—whether it be morality, doctrine, or obedience—results in spiritual instability. Preaching against sin while secretly engaging in it makes one a transgressor in the eyes of God, regardless of titles, wealth, or influence. Such duplicity renders one ineffective and susceptible to collapse under God's refining fire.

Paul's warning in Galatians 1:8-10 is clear: altering God's Word to suit personal desires or to please others is dangerous and unacceptable. The gospel cannot be manipulated to accommodate sin. Any attempt to rebuild a life on compromised principles is destined for failure, much like constructing with hay that will not withstand the test of fire.

Paul's admonition in 2 Corinthians 13:5 urges us to *"Examine yourselves, whether ye be in the faith."* Self-examination is vital. Are you building with materials that will endure? Have you compromised God's Word for convenience or worldly acceptance?

Lord, give us the grace to remain steadfast in Your Word. Help us to examine our hearts and remove every trace of compromise. Strengthen us to build with materials that will endure Your testing. Keep us faithful to the very end. In Jesus' name, Amen.

May God bless you and keep your spiritual edifice standing strong on the foundation of Christ. Amen.

ABOUT THE AUTHOR

Oluwagbemi Joshua Olusesan is a devout follower of Christ, born into the esteemed family of Reverend Samuel Oluwagbemi (formerly known as Osanyingbemi) in Iyin, Ekiti State, Nigeria, located in West Africa. He pursued his education at the School of Metallurgical and Materials Engineering in The Federal Polytechnic Idah, graduating in 1996 as part of the esteemed graduate set. As a passionate member of the Nigeria Metallurgical Society, he has actively contributed to his field.

In the year 1990, Oluwagbemi Joshua Olusesan committed his life to Christ Jesus, marking a significant turning point. Since then, he has been steadfastly immersed in the divine portal, experiencing the boundless love and mercy of God. His spiritual journey includes being an alumnus of CU NIFES Idah chapter, where he actively participated and contributed as the State Publicity Secretary in 1997. During this time, he penned his first national article titled "From Jerusalem to Jericho," which garnered recognition and appreciation.

Furthermore, Oluwagbemi Joshua Olusesan received spiritual enrichment through his involvement in various institutions. In 1998, he completed the WOFBI program conducted by Living Faith Church, further deepening his faith and understanding of the gospel. Additionally, he attended the Spiritual War College at MFM in 2000, expanding his spiritual knowledge and insights. In 2015, he became a member of RCCG, The Redeemed Christian Church Of God, and continued his spiritual growth under their guidance. To further augment his theological understanding, he pursued postgraduate studies at The Life Theological Seminary, Ikorodu, specializing in Mission and Church Growth, successfully completing the program in 2019.

As a prolific writer of the gospel, Oluwagbemi Joshua Olusesan has consistently shared his insights and inspirations with others. His writings reflect his deep faith and understanding of God's word, providing guidance and encouragement to readers. In his personal life, he finds immense joy and fulfillment in his marriage to Taiwo, and they are blessed with children who bring blessings and happiness to their home.

Recognizing his divine calling, Oluwagbemi Joshua Olusesan has been commissioned by God to engage in apostolic ministries, dedicating himself to spreading the message of Christ and empowering others through his spiritual endeavors.